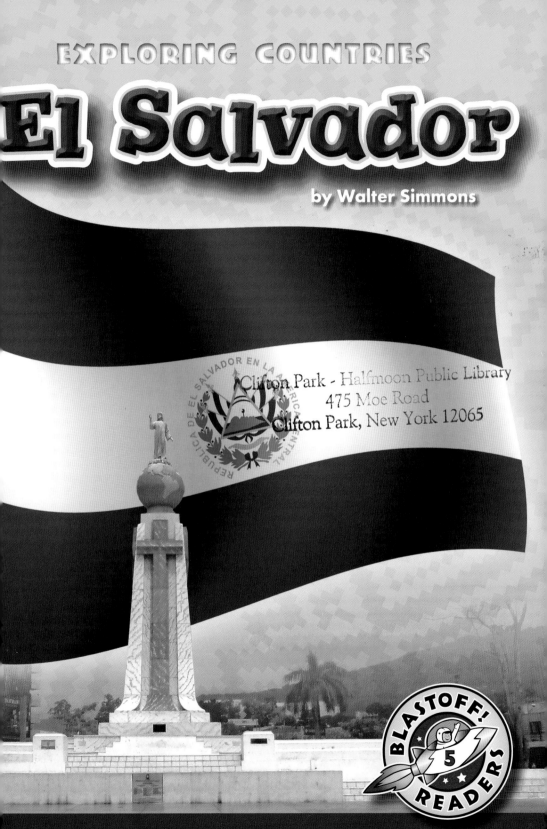

EXPLORING COUNTRIES

El Salvador

by Walter Simmons

BELLWETHER MEDIA • MINNEAPOLIS, MN

BLASTOFF! READERS 5

Note to Librarians, Teachers, and Parents:

Blastoff! Readers are carefully developed by literacy experts and combine standards-based content with developmentally appropriate text.

Level 1 provides the most support through repetition of high-frequency words, light text, predictable sentence patterns, and strong visual support.

Level 2 offers early readers a bit more challenge through varied simple sentences, increased text load, and less repetition of high-frequency words.

Level 3 advances early-fluent readers toward fluency through increased text and concept load, less reliance on visuals, longer sentences, and more literary language.

Level 4 builds reading stamina by providing more text per page, increased use of punctuation, greater variation in sentence patterns, and increasingly challenging vocabulary.

Level 5 encourages children to move from "learning to read" to "reading to learn" by providing even more text, varied writing styles, and less familiar topics.

Whichever book is right for your reader, Blastoff! Readers are the perfect books to build confidence and encourage a love of reading that will last a lifetime!

9841

This edition first published in 2012 by Bellwether Media, Inc.

No part of this publication may be reproduced in whole or in part without written permission of the publisher. For information regarding permission, write to Bellwether Media, Inc., Attention: Permissions Department, 5357 Penn Avenue South, Minneapolis, MN 55419.

Library of Congress Cataloging-in-Publication Data
Simmons, Walter.
  El Salvador / by Walter Simmons.
    p. cm. – (Blastoff! readers: exploring countries)
  Includes bibliographical references and index.
  Summary: "Developed by literacy experts for students in grades three through seven, this book introduces young readers to the geography and culture of El Salvador"–Provided by publisher.
  ISBN 978-1-60014-730-2 (hardcover : alk. paper)
  1. El Salvador–Juvenile literature. I. Title.
  F1483.2 .S56
  972.84–dc23   2011032006

Printed in the United States of America, North Mankato, MN.

010112   1203

Contents

Guatemala

Honduras

El Salvador

★ San Salvador

Gulf of Fonseca

Pacific Ocean

N
W   E
S

Did you know?

El Salvador is the only country in Central America that does not touch the Caribbean Sea.

Nicaragua

El Salvador is the smallest country in Central America, covering only 8,124 square miles (21,041 square kilometers). San Salvador, its capital and largest city, is located in the western half of the country. In the north, El Salvador borders Honduras and Guatemala. To the south, El Salvador has a long coastline on the Pacific Ocean. The **Gulf** of Fonseca sits at the southeastern corner of El Salvador. This gulf also touches Nicaragua and Honduras.

Parque Nacional El Imposible

fun fact

El Salvador has a national park named *Parque Nacional El Imposible*. This means "Impossible National Park" in Spanish. The park surrounds a deep gorge that is very difficult and dangerous to travel through.

El Salvador is a mountainous country. The Sierra Madre range runs near the border with Honduras in the north. This range includes Cerro El Pital, the highest point in El Salvador. The peak reaches a height of 8,957 feet (2,730 meters). In the east, the Goascorán River separates El Salvador and Honduras. The Lempa is El Salvador's largest river and the only river wide and deep enough to allow the passage of ships.

A central plain lies between the Sierra Madre and a series of **volcanoes** in the south. Ancient volcanic eruptions left fields of black **lava** rock in this hilly plain. In a few places, underground hot springs erupt in small **geysers**. Some volcanoes are still active, and earthquakes often strike El Salvador.

El Salvador lies on top of a deep underground **fault**. More than twenty volcanoes rise on the land above this fault. Some of these vent hot lava and steam from underneath the surface of the earth.

El Salvador's tallest volcano is Ilamatepec. It rises 7,749 feet (2,362 meters) in the western mountains. Another name for this volcano is Santa Ana, as the town of Santa Ana lies nearby. The volcano last erupted in 2005. Smoke poured from the mountaintop while volcanic rock flew several miles into the air. Some of the rocks were as big as cars!

Santa Ana

blue-and-gold
macaws

emerald boa
constrictor

fun fact

El Salvador is home to the
Mexican hairy dwarf porcupine.
This tough rodent has sharp spines
and can use its tail to climb and
grab food.

The forests of El Salvador shelter a variety of
tropical birds and insects. El Salvador has 20
different hummingbirds and hundreds of butterfly
species. Colorful macaws, toucans, and quetzals
brighten treetops.

monarch
butterfly

Alligators and crocodiles live in the country's coastal **lagoons**. Several dangerous snakes, including the pit viper and boa constrictor, slither around in search of prey. Sharks, tuna, and dolphins swim in the coastal waters. The Pacific coast is also home to several kinds of sea turtles, including the hawksbill and the leatherback.

Did you know?

El Salvador is the most crowded country in Central America. There are about 750 people per square mile, or 290 per square kilometer.

About 6 million people live in El Salvador. They are called Salvadorans. Nine out of every ten Salvadorans are *mestizos*. Their **ancestors** are **Amerindians** and Europeans.

A small Amerindian population still lives in El Salvador. Most of these Amerindians belong to the Pipil people. They live in western El Salvador and speak the Nahua language. Communities of **immigrants** from Nicaragua, Honduras, and Guatemala also live in El Salvador. Most immigrants live in San Salvador and other cities. Spanish is the official language of El Salvador, and it is spoken by most Salvadorans.

Speak Spanish!

English	Spanish	How to say it
hello	hola	OH-lah
good-bye	adios	ah-dee-OHS
yes	sí	SEE
no	no	NOH
please	por favor	POHR fah-VOR
thank you	gracias	GRAH-see-uhs
friend (male)	amigo	ah-MEE-goh
friend (female)	amiga	ah-MEE-gah

Did you know?
Salvadorans like to decorate the walls of buildings in their cities with murals. The bright, vibrant murals reflect the Salvadoran culture.

Most city-dwellers in El Salvador live in apartments, often with many of their relatives. During the day, people take buses to work or the market. In the evening, they often walk to a **plaza** to meet friends and chat.

Life is different in the countryside. Many homes are made of clay bricks, dried mud, and straw. Some families have a *parcela*, or a plot of land to grow their own food. To get around, people walk or share vehicles. The ride can be rough over the bumpy country roads.

Where People Live in El Salvador

countryside
36%

cities
64%

In El Salvador, most children attend kindergarten through grade nine. After grade nine, high schools offer two more years of classes. High school students study history, geography, math, and science. **Vocational schools** teach useful skills and prepare students for future jobs.

School can be expensive. Classes are free, but families must pay for school supplies. Many children stay home and work instead of attending school. In the countryside, many towns and villages have no schools at all.

Did you know?

Salvadoran students always wear a uniform. White shirts and dark pants or skirts are standard.

Did you know?

Salvadorans used to earn and spend *colones*. In 2001, the country dropped this currency and now uses the U.S. dollar.

Where People Work in El Salvador

manufacturing 23%

services 58%

farming 19%

In the cities of El Salvador, most people hold **service jobs**. They work in shops, banks, hotels, restaurants, and other businesses that provide services. Other workers earn a living from factory work. They make shoes, clothing, and household goods. Some factories are *maquiladoras*, which only make goods for foreign companies. Food factories process sugarcane, coffee beans, and other farm crops.

In the countryside, most farmers work on big **plantations**. They tend and harvest crops such as coffee beans and sugarcane. On the coast, fishers net shrimp, lobster, and other seafood.

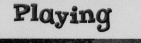

Soccer is the number one sport in El Salvador. Every major city and town has a soccer field where local kids play. Salvadorans also enjoy surfing and boxing. Surfing is big along the seacoast. Large waves swell and break at Punta Roca, the most popular surfing spot. The many volcanoes of El Salvador offer hiking and scenic views.

After school, kids play tag and hide-and-seek. Salvadoran girls enjoy a game called *el reloj*, which means "the clock." They form a circle of twelve around one girl. This girl swings a long jump rope along the ground. Everyone else has to jump over it and call out numbers in order. If the rope hits a girl, or she calls out the wrong number, she's out.

Did you know?

Meat is expensive for many Salvadorans. Instead of beef or chicken, they may enjoy a meal of freshly caught iguana or armadillo!

pupusa

Salvadorans usually eat a simple breakfast of coffee and bread. Lunch is the biggest meal of the day. Many people enjoy stuffed pastries called *empanadas*. Another favorite is *pupusas*. These are thick corn tortillas filled with meat, cheese, rice, or beans.

In the evening, meals are lighter. Rice and beans are popular. Cooks flavor stews and soups with ground pumpkin or sesame seeds. Sweet cakes and fruits are favorite desserts. Salvadorans also enjoy *atol*, a thick drink made from boiled corn. Some *atol* is so thick you need a spoon to eat it!

empanadas

atol

Independence Day

In El Salvador, Independence Day takes place on September 15. This holiday celebrates the country's freedom from Spanish rule in 1821. Floats follow the main streets of cities, and school bands play. Salvadoran workers parade through the streets on May 1 to celebrate Labor Day.

Salvadorans celebrate *El Salvador del Mundo* in August. Festivities honor Jesus Christ, the country's **patron saint**. People crowd into the capital for ceremonies and concerts. Christmas and *Semana Santa,* the holy week leading up to Easter, are other important religious holidays in El Salvador. Salvadorans often act out events from the life of Jesus on these holidays.

! fun fact

November 2 is the Day of the Dead. On this day, people across Latin America honor the dead by painting graves and dressing as skeletons. Some even make candy skulls!

candy skulls

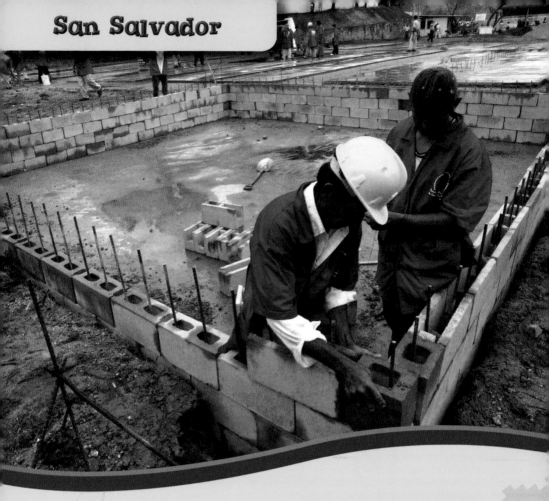

San Salvador is the capital and largest city of El Salvador. Earthquakes, floods, and other natural disasters have destroyed the city multiple times. However, the people of San Salvador have always found a way to rebuild their beloved city.

At the center of San Salvador is a **monument** showing Jesus Christ atop a globe. In 1986, an earthquake damaged this monument. Workers were quick to put the monument back together. Today, Salvadorans view it as a symbol of their culture.

Did you know?

The monument's official name is Monumento al Divino Salvador del Mundo, or "Monument to the Savior of the World."

Fast Facts About El Salvador

El Salvador's Flag

The flag of El Salvador is blue with a horizontal band of white through the middle. White stands for peace, and blue stands for justice. In the center of the flag is the national coat of arms and the name *Republica de El Salvador en la America Central*, which means "the Republic of El Salvador in Central America."

Official Name: Republic of El Salvador

Area: 8,124 square miles
(21,041 square kilometers);
El Salvador is the 153rd largest
country in the world.

Capital City:	San Salvador
Important Cities:	Acajutla, Sonsonate, Santa Ana, San Miguel
Population:	6,071,774 (July 2011)
Official Language:	Spanish
National Holiday:	Independence Day (September 15)
Religions:	Christian (78.3%), None (16.8%), Other (4.9%)
Major Industries:	farming, fishing, manufacturing, services
Natural Resources:	hydropower, fertile land, oil
Manufactured Products:	textiles, clothing, furniture, fertilizers, food products, beverages
Farm Products:	coffee beans, sugarcane, sugar beets, corn, rice, beans, oilseed, cotton, sorghum, beef, dairy products
Unit of Money:	U.S. dollar; the dollar is divided into 100 cents.

Glossary

Amerindians—peoples originally from North, South, or Central America

ancestors—relatives who lived long ago

fault—a break in a layer of rock deep underground

geysers—natural fountains of hot water and steam from underground

gulf—part of an ocean or sea that extends into land

immigrants—people who leave one country to live in another

lagoons—small, shallow bodies of water connected to larger bodies of water

lava—hot, melted rock that flows out of an active volcano

monument—a statue or artwork designed to mark an important place, person, or event

patron saint—a saint who is believed to look after a country or group of people

plantations—large farms that grow coffee beans, cotton, sugarcane, or other crops; plantations are mainly located in warmer climates.

plaza—a large square in the center of a town or city

service jobs—jobs that perform tasks for people or businesses

species—specific kinds of living things; members of a species share the same characteristics.

vocational schools—schools that train students to do specific jobs

volcanoes—holes in the earth; when a volcano erupts, lava shoots out.

To Learn More

AT THE LIBRARY

DiPiazza, Francesca Davis. *El Salvador in Pictures*. Minneapolis, Minn.: Twenty-First Century Books, 2008.

Foley, Erin, and Rafiz Hapipi. *El Salvador*. New York, N.Y.: Marshall Cavendish Benchmark, 2005.

Shields, Charles J. *El Salvador*. Broomall, Pa.: Mason Crest Publishers, 2009.

ON THE WEB

Learning more about El Salvador is as easy as 1, 2, 3.

1. Go to www.factsurfer.com.

2. Enter "El Salvador" into the search box.

3. Click the "Surf" button and you will see a list of related Web sites.

With factsurfer.com, finding more information is just a click away.

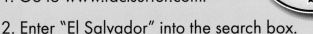

Index